always know just how much I adore you

Heaven Mendez

BookLeaf Publishing

India | USA | UK

Presentation by *BookLeaf Publishing*

Web: www.bookleafpub.com

E-mail: info@bookleafpub.com

ISBN: 9789360946807

First edition 2024

my mother, Rosa Lee.

I feel you'd appreciate this.

ACKNOWLEDGEMENT

Anyone and everyone who has played some part in this journey, whether it be an English teacher, cool mentor, or a friend.

also all the therapists. They're cool too.

PREFACE

Okay, this is that book that I swore I would write in middle school, then again in high school, and again in college. I'm not quite sure what started this, but it's been therapeutic. I was always arguably the worst at poetry because nothing I say ever rhymes, nor does it seem to elicit any strong emotions in either direction, but it's cool to see how much I've evolved not just as a writer, but as a human being.

So I present to you, this terrible amalgamation of silly thoughts and ideas, stemming from one very depressed teenager, all the way to an equally confused adult trying her best. It's much easier to laugh and learn than it is to keep everything under wraps. I hope this makes even one person laugh, even if it's that semi-fake polite laugh someone does when it's kind of funny, but not enough to warrant genuine laughter.

Cheers, friends.

the sweet illusion

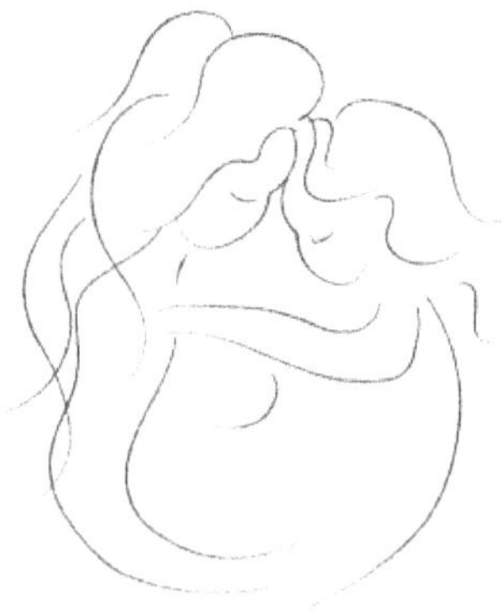

she's sweet.
like smooth caramel kisses,
guides the world with her divine,
thoughts of grandeur,
she exists in a world of candy-coated deceit,
like snowflakes in summer,
like shooting stars,
like euphoria,
she knows no bounds.

and I can't let her go.
no matter how good it feels.

A Farewell's Lost Moment

sorry, I said bye.
took too long to realize.
you had gone away.

third-degree burns

ashes to ashes, we all fall down,
ambers to embers, sparking a flame,
peaking and burning at the sound of your name.

a plague of existence that calls you it's home,
considers you weak as you're destined to be
alone,
you've fallen through bridges you burned on
your own.

each place is numbered, each member recasted,
retracted once the scene is adapted,
your worth is nothing more than cinders.

I'd rather be caught in the flame,
then the fiery compress of your selfish
misdemeanor,
I would gladly catch fire than have to deal with
any more of your pain.

they say blue burns the hottest, and while that
may be true,
it's never been the brightest.

don't underestimate the embers.
one wrong move and you're sure to perish.

daddy issues

you smell like wasted dreams and parental
regret.
like too many late-night stands and a lack of
ambition.
you are sad. you are broken.
there's too much to be done.

you drink to forget but always remember
what it's like to be forgotten.
you are your favorite doll without a painted-on
smile.
unloved as soon as the next one comes out.

pillowy soft, pouty lips,
slim waist, small hips.
bust bigger than his wildest dreams.

pretty little pin-up girl.
untouchable.
daddy's little mistake. infeasible.

guess it was never meant to be.

sempiternal

you can tell from the look in my eyes that I'm
going nowhere,
each day on top of another, but you take one
phrase into assumption, and weeks could go by
without a single notch of determination from
either side.

I enjoy two things: watching them fall forward
in their own demise, and counting every moment
that I no longer feel alone.
keeping hopes high and heads down low, the
logic has been found in the very things you call
insignificant.

and yet, my hopes and dreams have as little to
do with reality as humanly possible.

has it graced you in the slightest that even the
highest means of escape don't always ensure an
exit
that sometimes seeing the end is as real as
finding solace in falling head first, six stories up.

the pretentious actions of those who see but
don't listen. who experience but don't cherish.

who fly before falling. sometimes, I'd rather just
fall.

life contradicts. the cycle goes on and on. I'd
rather be thrown into the fire.

release every nonexistent ounce of self-respect,
to the sky ablaze.

because this right here, is sempiternal.
and you'll never get to see the end.

not okay, I promise

there is a difference between looking and seeing
one without the other has no meaning
and even in the end apologies can't heal what's
already been lost

there are moments like this when sorry is taken
to the wrist, and the mind is left to wander
unseen,
but looks can be deceiving, and maybe this life
does, in fact, have no meaning but even the
words can't save me now.

lock me up, I'm insane.

psychosis of a lifestyle that has yet to be pulled
from fiction,
without a doubt, satire, I'm finished living in the
shadows

I may be heaven, but every ounce is plucked
from hell. I mean darkness.

there's not enough to shed light on a situation,
the way you can from blood or tears,
so just tell me:
if a broken child falls and no one wants to hear
it, does it make a sound?
to this day, that fate is mine. I'm not okay, I
promise.
so take your chemically induced romances and
leave me be.

I'm a lot more than a weak little medicine child.
But that's not what you want to hear, is it?

disposable

scars to you're beautiful,

because scars made you beautiful

expendable till it's commendable to be gone.

it's neither here nor there
that everyone seems to care,
once one's self succumbs to despair.

you're not sorry,
you're caught,
you're not grieving,
you're distraught,
you could get away with this,
or so you thought.

deception is a misconception when clouded by a
lover's perception

you've scarred her and now she's beautiful.

beautiful because she's gone.

waiting for the shout

I miss mom hugs

I miss mom laughs and smiles and the judgy
looks from poor choices, the audible sigh before
problems become late night adventures and
lectures and promises that things will get a little
better.

I miss feeling safe,
of feeling like even if there was no one else, at
least she was there, maybe she cared, but even if
she couldn't be mom, we could still be friends.

I see her face when she's sleeping, but the kind
of sleep where there're dreams and breathing,
that I can take solace in the fact that if I make

too much noise she'll wake up and yell at me.
God, why isn't she yelling at me, please just yell
at me.

say something so I know you're still out there.

maybe it's supposed to be this way,
feeling lonely and unloved,
because it's what I deserve.
I ruined her, I didn't deserve her.

she's not like other girls,
she's dead-
-set on making sure everyone knows she's gone-
-out for a while because she couldn't make it to
the end-
-of her life.

she's not like other girls,

she was my mom.

on city streets and stars

I assure you, no harm will come,
The weak-minded and foul-hearted pay no
attention to the ones bringing strength into a
world that's lost its luster.
diamonds cannot shine without the perfect idea
in mind,
it was you who ruined the sadness.

we parade ourselves on rooftops, staring down
those that are lesser,
wanting a better life for ourselves, yet we are the
very means to survival.
we slept on city streets on winter nights,
hoping for the blessed something to take the
dullness from our eyes,
and you, you've taken away from it this time.

we can't all be stars, but those who can
eventually fall,
shunned by ego, by mind-gaping nuances,
there is no need for individuals, as we're
supposed to be whole.

you can't feel correctly if your mind scatters
from six seconds to six years, and even then
there's no release.
God help those who cannot see, those who
cannot be, and all those righteous for the
damned.
we see with our hearts but not with our minds.

In time, we lose sight of what really matters,
but what if it doesn't at all?

Who takes the fall for?
who wants nothing more than to die in a familiar
wasteland?
We don't want you; you take up too much space.

let the blood of those who don't believe, who
can't understand, drench my hands and flow
forward, to the edges of the earth, where no one
can find them.

we convey what we aspire into excuses
we look for evidence in these city streets,

brimming with what actually lies there.
despaired and alone, we fight to defend the little
we actually have, and we enjoy it.
It is you, my friend, who has lost the magic.

In the Silence After

in the eclipsed silence of your last choice,
I find words,
a raucous cavalcade of the irreverent,
spilling like uninvited guests through the
doorway
of my splintered restraint.

you left,
not with the hushed reverence of a sunset
but with the abruptness of a curtain's fall
in the middle of an act.
and here I am, standing in the scattered applause
of memories, unsure if I should bow or leave the
stage.

I remember your laughter,
a sound that could dance on the wind,

tickle the leaves into a soft chuckle.
now, in the irony of your absence,
that laughter twists into a question mark,
punctuating the silence with its absence.

oh, how the profanity spills
a bastard language for a bastard feeling,
because what the fuck, Mom?
you dropped your pain like a coat in summer,
left it at my feet, and I can't help but trip over it
every goddamn day.

they say grief is just love with nowhere to go,
so I build a shrine of expletives and side-eyes,
a holy place for the unholy feelings
because you were never one for church pews or
stained glass.
you were more of a stained-glass soul
a kaleidoscope of sharp edges and light.

I am the archeologist of our shared history,
dusting off the fragments you left behind,
piecing together the mosaic of a woman
a mother, who wore sarcasm-like armor
and wielded humor like a sword.

I imagine you chuckling,
a ghostly sound that haunts the corners of my
mind,

as I navigate the minefield of your parting gift,
each step an irreverent dance with fate.
did you know that your final act
would turn my world into a tragicomedy?

in the quiet, I confront the taboo,
the jokes that bubble up from the abyss,
dark humor that you'd appreciate
with a smirk and a sip of something strong.
but the laugh catches in my throat,
a prisoner of circumstance and sorrow.

your honesty, a sharp tool,
slices through the bullshit,
yet it's that same brutal honesty
that whispers to me at night,
reminding me of the questions left unanswered,
of the love left unspoken.

they say to speak of the dead as they lived,
so I raise a toast to you,
with a quip on my lips and a tear in my eye,
to the woman who taught me to question the
world,
to laugh in its face and yet embrace it tightly.

in the end, you left as you lived —
on your own fucking terms.
and while I'm left sifting through the debris,

I find solace in the fragments of your truth,
in the funny, sarcastic, profane, honest ramblings
that are the map to the treasure of you.

so here's to the words unfiltered,
to the love, complex and unscripted,
to a life lived loud and without apology,
and to a departure that left us all speechless,
except for me, with my ramblings,
trying to find the punchline
in a joke that never quite lands.

From Fairytales to Falling Apart

dear little dreamer with starry eyes and heart
aglow,
forgive me, for I have wandered far from the
path
you painted in hues of hero's valor and fairytale
endings.
you sketched out lives in the margins of
dog-eared pages
bold knights, wise wizards, and the
sharp-shooting rogues
each a pledge, a promise to your tender, waiting
self.

in the tapestry of your mind, they stood, gallant
and true,
and you wove them into the fabric of your
destiny,
a destiny I have since unraveled thread by silver
thread.
how you believed in the gentle touch of the
prince's hand,
the rogue's smirking rescue from towers
unnumbered,
and the wizard's wise words weaving a magic so
pure.

with every turn of the page, every flicker of the
screen,
a new love bloomed, a heart-shaped bubble of
innocence.
you pledged your troth to these phantoms of ink
and light,
each one a whispered vow beneath the
cottonwood tree.
oh, how you danced with them in dreams,
their faces, a revolving masquerade of perfect
love.

yet here we stand, in the stark light of grown-up
days,
where no parchment holds the key to
forevermore.

the swords have rusted; the spells have lost their
charm,
and the roguish grins are now but echoes in the
void.
youth's sweet crushes, a carousel of imagined
kisses,
left behind in the attic of your being, gathering
dust.

I have tried, little one, to find their flesh and
bone counterparts,
but the quest has been a wild goose chase in
glass slippers
that never quite fit. The clock has struck its
midnight toll,
and I am left with pumpkin shards and mice that
never were stallions.
the world, it turns out, is an unscripted drama,
no scripted entrances, no curtain calls, no written
finales.

so I come before you, a penitent with empty
hands,
bearing the weight of unmet dreams and the
absence of fables.
I've sought heroes in the alleys and castles of
reality,
only to find them wanting, lacking, just shy of
legend.

the apologies hang in the air, a fog of
what-could-have-beens,
and the truth, a bitter potion I must now serve
you,

men are trash.

happy pills and psychiatrist bills

pill bottle rattles,
empty as my serotonin,
oops, brain's on vacation.

morning's usual guest,
forgot to refill, oh yes,
grey clouds in my chest.

pharmacy trip skipped,
now my mood's doing backflips,
laughter on eclipse.

brain's chemical dance,

missed a beat, lost in trance,
give my joy a chance.

doc's number on speed,
need a refill, yes indeed,
happy thoughts, proceed.

smile's on layaway,
pills will bring it back to play,
whoops, laugh another day.

mood's a bumpy ride,
without meds, can't hide inside,
laughter, coincide?

an echo of resolve

in the vast theater of naysayers' chorus,
I danced alone, a solitary defiance,
amidst the cacophony of can'ts and won'ts,
their words, barbed arrows meant to tether my
spirit.

oh, you architects of doubt, bricklayers of
despair,
you, who wear skepticism as crowns,
and wield discouragement as scepters,
to you, I offer a bouquet of my tenacity.

I am not the clay in your weary, cynical hands,
not a sculpture to shape with your limiting
beliefs,
you, so generous with your prophecies of failure,

so stingy with the currency of faith.

to the teachers who saw a mind too wild,
a canvas too vibrant for your monochrome
dreams,
I paint my life in strokes of rebellion,
a mural of achievements too grand for your
narrow halls.

to the relatives who spoke the language of the
ordinary,
who urged the safe path, the beaten road, the
subdued ambition,
I charted courses in unexplored skies,
steering by stars you claimed were extinguished.

to the lovers who doubted a heart could hold
dreams so vast,
who feared being eclipsed by the glow of my
aspirations,
I became the sun, fierce and unapologetic,
and you, merely shadows of a forgotten eclipse.

to the friends who smirked at the audacity of my
goals,
who whispered bets on my downfall at every
bold leap I took,
I gambled on myself, and the dice rolled to
victory,

while your laughter faded into the silence of my
ascent.

and to the echo of my own voice, during
moments of falter,
when I parroted your poison, doubting the
strength in my bones,
I found resolve in my reflection, a steadfast ally,
I learned to shout over the storm of your
collective scorn.

with every triumph carved from the bedrock of
my will,
I sent a reverberation, a seismic wave of
defiance,
an earthquake to the foundations of your
disbelief,
a huge proverbial "fuck you," resounding
through the rubble of your scorn.

I am the living testament, a legend self-scripted,
my flesh and blood the manuscript of
perseverance,
your doubt, the chisel that sculpted my resolve,
my success, the epitaph on the tombstone of
your "cannot."

I am the crescendo rising from the whispers of
impossibility,

a symphony of "I can" and "I did," a harmony of
self-belief,
you, the dissonant note fading into the past,
a footnote in my chapters of conquest and
self-realization.

so to all who've ever told me I couldn't,
thank you for the fuel, for the fire, for the flight,
for in telling me I couldn't,
you ignited the inferno of a soul who knew it
could.

the plot twist we all wanted

iron bars embrace,
your new home fits like a glove,
warmest regards, dad.

cell block serenades,
whispers of your fatherhood
echo, then they fade.

concrete hugs you tight,
while freedom toasts to your health,
cheers, with every night.

prison's cold caress,
a father's love, absentee,
I thrive nonetheless.

justice serves you well,
in orange, you're quite the sight,
stories I won't tell.

enjoy your stay, Sir,
your absence, a sweet relief,
life's fine without you.

walls hear my laughter,
time's up for you, hereafter,
I rise, you falter.

clink of chains, so sweet,
melody of your defeat,
karma's tune, upbeat.

no tears on my cheek,
your power, once strong, now weak,
my future, not bleak.

hate, a heavy stone,
dropped in letters, left alone,
my heart, now full-grown.

you're gone energy,
fueled by your memory,
I'm free, endlessly.

may jailhouse whispers,

remind you, fall's brisk twisters,
I thrive, you wither.

in cells of despair,
recall, I was under your care,
now, breathe stagnant air.

your great time, my hope,
choked by justice's tight rope,
in darkness, you grope.

forged in your disdain,
a phoenix from the pain,
I break every chain.

enjoy your small room,
while I, in full bloom,
dance away the gloom.

coffee cream and silly dreams

in the sultry swelter of a July morning,
you stand, a silhouette against the dawnlight,
cool and collected, a presence unwavering.
your essence, a soothing whisper upon my lips,
a touch that chills the sleep from my bones,
and in your depths, I find the clarity of daybreak.

your arms, long and slender, wrap around the
city's pulse,
a cascade of comfort in a cup, the glass sweats
with the burden of your embrace, a condensation
of care.
dark as the fertile earth, rich with hidden secrets,
your body, a bittersweet canvas of energy, swirls

with the promise of alertness, of moments stolen
from slumber.

your breath, a fragrance that dances through the
air,
hints of caramel and cocoa, a distant memory of
heat,
now tamed by ice, by your calm composure.
you speak in cool sips, a language of
refreshment,
a dialect of morning necessity, and I am fluent
in your silent conversation, your caffeinated
communion.

a laugh bubbles up as the sun climbs higher,
the world awakening to your gentle insistence.
you do not shout, you do not demand,
you are the understated proclamation of a new
day,
a confidant to the sleepy and the overworked,
a companion to the lonely hearts at dawn.

your shadow stretches across my table, a
constant guardian,
And I wonder, how is it that something so cold
can infuse such warmth into the fabric of my
day?
how is it that you, without a word, without a
heartbeat,

can be the most intimate friend in this room of
strangers?

and as the clock ticks on, my reliance on you
grows,
a dependency I jest at, but secretly revere.
you are the ritual that steadies shaking hands,
the liquid courage that emboldens a weary spirit.

and here I sit, enamored by your icy touch,
lost in the company of your silent affirmation.
a devotion so strong,
that it makes me chuckle at my own expense,
for who needs the warmth of another's arms
when I have your chilled embrace to hold me
tight?

and yet, despite your constancy, your
unwavering chill,
I must admit, with a self-deprecating grin,
that while you may keep my cup forever full,
you'll never leave me quite as breathless
as a lover's kiss might, for you see,
my heart may race, but it's only the caffeine.

9/14

in a crumpled piece of paper,
words scrawled in haste,
unfiltered, unapologetic,
a release of pent-up emotions
that I never knew existed.

my mother's note,
a jumble of thoughts and feelings,
a puzzle left unfinished,
but her words,
they strike a chord within me,
at bittersweet melody
of love and regret.

I laugh at the absurdity
of her choice of words,
the random expletives
sprinkled like confetti
on a somber occasion,
and yet,
they bring a smile to my face,
a reminder of her irreverent spirit
that lives on in me.

I reach for the phone,
to call her and share a joke,
but the dial tone mocks me,
a reminder of her absence,
a void that cannot be filled.

so I sit with her note,
tears and laughter intertwined,
a strange mix of emotions
that only a mother could evoke.
and in that moment,
I feel her presence,
not in the paper,
but in the memories
that we shared,
in the love that will never fade.

thirty-something or other

in the mirror, I see the lines of time etched
across my face, a map of missed chances
I stand on the brink of thirty, a decade
of dreams unfulfilled, goals left abandoned

I hear the whispers of doubt, the taunts
of my inner critic, mocking my failures
I am a vessel of unmet expectations, a shadow
of the person I thought I would become

I berate myself for the wasted days, the moments
squandered on frivolous pursuits, the years
slipped through my fingers like sand in a desert
I am a barren landscape, devoid of
accomplishment

but in this moment of self-flagellation, I pause
and see the beauty in the broken pieces
I am a work in progress, a canvas
waiting to be painted with new beginnings

I may not have reached the heights of success
but I am still standing, still breathing
and that in itself is an accomplishment
I am not defined by my failures but by my
resilience

so I will embrace the uncertainty of the future
with open arms and a hopeful heart
for I am not limited by my past mistakes
I am a phoenix rising from the ashes of
self-doubt.

ace of hearts

in a world of lust,
I'm just here like, "Hmm, nope,"
love is not my jam.

desire eludes me,
confusion reigns supreme here,
but hey, less drama.

hearts flutter and ache,
but mine stays calm and steady,
just give me some cake.

labels are tricky,
I'll just be me, no big deal,
who needs all that stress?

so here I stand proud,

in my own unique glory,
confused but content.

in a world of lust,
I'm lost in a sea of thoughts,
where's the instruction?

desire's a riddle,
my compass points to nowhere,
lost in the puzzle.

romance is a maze,
I navigate with caution,
where's the exit sign?

love's a foreign land,
I'm a tourist with no map,
lost in translation.

heal

heal from mommy and
daddy issues, they said with
a sprinkle of sarcasm

as if a Band-Aid
could mend the wounds they unknowingly
left behind, oh so casually

just smile and nod,
and pretend their words
didn't slice through your soul

but here we are,
picking up the pieces
without a manual

healing is messy,
no quick fix for the mess
they left in their wake

so let's laugh it off,
embrace the chaos and
find our own way back to peace.

liquid serenade

in the stillness of night,
when the world slumbers
and dreams dance in the shadows,
there is a quiet magic
in the taste of solitude.

the darkness wraps around me,
a comforting shroud
that whispers of secrets
and untold stories.
in this sacred hour,
time stands still
and my soul awakens.

I am filled with a longing
for something unknown,
a yearning that pulls me

into the depths of my being.
and in the silence,
I find solace
in the taste of the unseen,
the essence of existence
that lingers on my lips.

it is a sweetness
that cannot be described,
a sensation that lingers
in the corners of my mind.
and in this moment,
I am free
to savor the wonder
of the universe
in all its mystery.

interlude

to the girl with the bright eyes,
who felt the world fall apart,
one day you'll be free.

I'm sorry, little one
for all the tears I didn't wipe away

I wish I could go back and tell you
it will be okay, that you will make it through
that every scar will make you stronger

but instead, here we are
two souls separated by time and experience
still trying to find our way home

absentee icons

another day, another excuse
to plaster smiles and fake gratitude,
to dredge up memories of a man
who may or may not deserve the pedestal.

we'll toast to the patriarchs,
the kings of half-assed existence,
of absentee affection,
all in the name of tradition.

let's celebrate the stoic figures,
the ones that taught us
emotions are for the weak
and vulnerability is a sin

here's to the ones who vanished,
leaving behind hollow echoes,
of what could've been,
and scars that never fade.

oh, how delightful it is,
to dedicate an entire day,
to those who left us wanting,
yearning for something more.
so let's raise our glasses,
to the bastions of masculinity,
to outdated ideals,
and empty gestures.

cheers to the fathers,
may their legacy live on,
in disappointment, depression,
in suicide attempts, self-harm,
and may they have the day they deserve.

unbound resolve

in this life, I've drawn my lines,
laid-out boundaries clear as day.
I refuse to be shackled
by societal expectations,
by the incessant ticking
of biological clocks.

I won't sacrifice my freedom
for the sake of convention,
Won't bow to the pressure
of perpetuating a lineage
I never signed up for.

let them raise their eyebrows,
let them whisper behind their hands.
I'll stand firm in my decision,
unapologetic, unyielding.

My time, my energy, my damn sanity—
they're mine to keep,
mine to cherish,
not to squander on obligations
I never asked for.

I'll chart my own path,
forge my own destiny,
and if that means walking alone,
so be it.

I won't trade my dreams
for a crib and a diaper bag,
won't sacrifice my aspirations
on the altar of parenthood.

so let them judge,
let them scoff,
I'll remain steadfast,
a rebel in a world
obsessed with conformity.

sanctimonious serenade

preaching righteousness,
yet their actions reek of bile,
veiled in holy guise.

with sanctimony,
they shield their insincerity,
blind to their folly.

their tongues drip with lies,
twisting scripture to excuse
their selfish whims.

but beneath the façade,
lies a well of arrogance,
overflowing with sin.

they wield religion
like a weapon, justifying
their irritating ways.

yet truth will expose
their charade, revealing the
emptiness within.

whispers of yesterday

in the entanglement of my mind,
memories and fantasies intertwine,
like vines creeping through an ancient ruin.

I wander through corridors of nostalgia,
where the past dances with the present,
and reality blurs into a Technicolor dream.

I'm a child again, chasing fireflies
in the backyard at dusk,
the air thick with the scent of freshly cut grass.

or I'm on a road trip with friends,
windows down, music blasting,
carefree laughter echoing through the car.

I'm lying in a field of wildflowers,
watching clouds morph into fantastical
creatures,
while the sun paints the sky in hues of orange
and pink.

But amidst the reverie and bliss,
there's a whisper of longing,
a yearning to stay lost in this reverie forever.
so I'll keep wandering through my dreams,
chasing echoes of moments past,
because in this world of make-believe,
I can be anything I want to be,
but I wish I could never wake up.

melodious melancholy

there's a heaviness in the air,
a weight that settles upon my shoulders
like a blanket of lead.

I sit in silence,
the minutes tick by
with agonizing slowness.

There's nothing to do,
nothing to see,
nothing to feel but the emptiness
that gnaws at my insides.

I watch the world pass by
in a blur of monotony,
each moment blending into the next

in a dull, colorless haze.

I try to fill the void
with mindless distractions,
but they only serve
to deepen the ache within me.

I long for something,
anything,
to break the monotony,
to breathe life into this stale existence.

But as the tears fall
and the emptiness consumes me,
I realize that sometimes
the saddest stories
are the ones left untold.

insult to humanity

oh, the irony of it all,
the absurdity of labeling
"fatherless behavior"
as some kind of insult.

as if my dear old dad,
the epitome of incompetence,
could ever be considered
a model of fatherhood.

his absence, a relief,
a break from the chaos
of his clumsy attempts
at being a parent.

"fatherless behavior," they say,
as if his presence would've made
any difference,
other than adding to the dysfunction.

so go ahead, world,
poke fun at my "fatherless behavior,"
for in truth, I'm better off
without his antics.

the fault is all mine

in the aftermath of absence,
there's a weight that settles
like a stone in the pit of my stomach.

I sift through memories
like ashes in the wind,
searching for clues,
for signs I might have missed.

Guilt hangs heavy in the air,
a constant companion
whispering accusations
of words left unsaid,
of actions left undone.

I replay conversations
like a broken record,
wondering if there was something
I could have said,
something I could have done
to change the outcome.

But the silence is deafening,
the answers elusive,
leaving me to drown

in a sea of regret
and what-ifs.

I carry the weight of guilt
like a burden on my shoulders,
a constant reminder
of a life lost
and the questions left unanswered.

the sardonic saga

well, there goes my fairy tale ending,
swirling down the drain
like last night's regrets.

I guess Prince Charming got lost
on his way to save me,
too busy rescuing damsels
who actually give a damn.

and the glass slipper?
Turns out it was a size too small,
just like my hopes and dreams.

so much for riding off into the sunset
on a majestic unicorn,
because let's face it,
my life's more like a train wreck
with no conductor in sight.

I'll trade my tiara for a bottle of wine,
and my castle for a studio apartment
with noisy neighbors
and questionable plumbing.

farewell to happily ever after,
hello to the reality check
that hits harder than a ton of bricks.

mornings and mayhem

in the daily ritual of awakening,
there's a familiar tug-of-war
between the craving for vitality
and the caution born of experience.

the allure of that first sip
beckons like a beacon in the morning haze,
promising a surge of vigor
to propel me through the day's challenges.

but beneath the surface lies
a quiet apprehension,
a recognition of the potential aftermath
that lurks within each cup.

so I approach with trepidation,
mindful of the fine line
between invigoration and excess,
knowing that in this delicate dance,
the steps must be taken with care.

less than

in the mirror's reflection,
I see a distortion of self,
a funhouse reflection
of flaws magnified,
imperfections amplified.

every curve, every line,
scrutinized under the harsh glare
of self-critique,
each blemish a dagger
in my already fragile sense of self.

I pick and prod,
trying to mold myself
into some semblance
of societal perfection,

but the more I try,
the further I stray
from acceptance.

I am a prisoner
of my own perception,
trapped in a never-ending
cycle of self-loathing
and self-scrutiny.
the weight of inadequacy
hangs heavy on my shoulders,
a burden I cannot shake,
a shadow that follows me
wherever I go.

I long to break free
from this prison of insecurity,
to see myself as I truly am—
flawed, yes,
but also worthy
of love and acceptance.

but for now,
I am trapped
in this hall of mirrors,
forever chasing
an unattainable ideal,
forever feeling
less than.

bruises and banter

ah, the folly of romanticizing
actions that wound instead of heal,
like applauding a demolition
for its artistic destruction.

to admire scars as badges
of honor,
and suffering as a mark
of depth,
is like praising a pothole
for its character.

but let's not kid ourselves,
there's no charm in self-inflicted wounds,
no sweetness in the aftermath
of reckless choices.

so let's drop the act,
and embrace the true beauty
of self-care and self-respect,
because nothing says "I love myself" quite like a
bandaged heart.

tonks

before you, she was a mystery,
a feline enigma with no name
to call her own.

whoever named her must have had
a sense of humor as twisted
as a corkscrew,
or perhaps they were simply
overwhelmed by her charm
and resorted to random syllables
strung together like a cat's cradle.

maybe they looked into her eyes
and saw galaxies swirling
in endless wonder,
or maybe they just glanced at her
and thought, "Yep, that's a cat."

but now she is yours,
and her name is a part of her,
etched into her very being
like a tattoo on her fur.

and while you may never understand
the logic behind her name,
it doesn't matter,
because to you, she is simply
your beloved cat,
regardless of what she's called.

divine dissonance

well, isn't that a cosmic joke,
my name, a celestial paradise
while my parents dance
in the depths of their own personal hells.

Heaven, they called me,
perhaps hoping to invoke
some divine intervention,
a sprinkling of grace
to counteract their misdeeds.

but alas, it seems the universe
has a wicked sense of humor,
bestowing me with a name
that shines like a beacon of purity
in the midst of their darkness.

so here I am,
a heavenly anomaly
in a family tree riddled
with rotten roots,
a living contradiction
that even the angels
must find amusing.

broken bouquets

in the sea of saccharine sentiments,
I wade through aisles adorned with roses,
trying to find a card that fits
the jagged edges of our relationship.

picturesque images of maternal bliss
mock me from their glossy frames,
reminding me of the chasm
that separates us.

I settle on a card, its words
as hollow as our conversations,
and sign my name with a bitter smile,
knowing that this gesture is as futile
as trying to paint over cracks in the foundation.

mother's day, a reminder
of what could have been,
of what should have been,
but instead, we're left
with this fractured semblance
of a mother-daughter bond.

so here's to you, Mom,
for all the missed opportunities
and broken promises,
for teaching me that love
is as complicated as it is fleeting.

clinically impaired

in the realm of test tubes and microscopes,
I tiptoe through the clinical lab
like a novice in a maze of mysteries,
trying to decipher the language of diagnostics
with the finesse of a toddler with a Rubik's cube.

each sample is a puzzle,
each result, a cryptic message
that I decipher with all the skill
of someone reading tea leaves.

I sit in meetings, surrounded by experts,
nodding along like I belong,
while inside, I'm trembling,
wondering when they'll realize
I'm just a charlatan in a lab coat.
cracking jokes to mask the panic
and the sinking feeling that maybe,
just maybe, I'm not cut out for this after all.

spiraling shadows

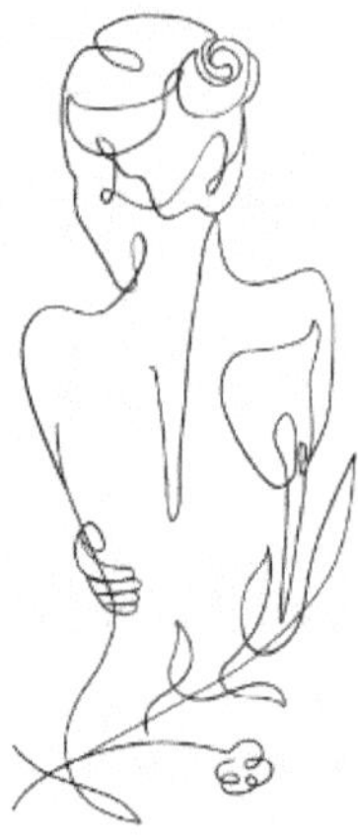

in shadows deep, the mirror reflects,
a canvas of doubts, where darkness collects.
fingers trace lines, etched with disdain,
a self-portrait painted in whispers of pain.

echoes dance within the hollowed halls,
where fractured fragments, the soul enthralls.
eyes meet eyes, in a silent lament,
lost in the maze where self-critiques ferment.

a spiral descends, a vortex unseen,
where whispers of inadequacy convene.
measured against shadows of who I should be,
a prisoner of comparison, never truly free.

each step forward, weighed by the past,
footprints of failures, a spell they cast.
in the dance of worth, I falter and fall,
lost in the symphony of self-inflicted
withdrawal.

unraveling threads of worth and of
worthlessness,
a tapestry torn in the grasp of distress.
in the silent chamber of self-condemnation's
sway,
I drown in the depths of a twilight's decay.

amidst the noise of a world's expectations,
I lose myself in endless self-flagellations.
in the maze of comparison's cruel design,
I suffocate beneath its weight, resigned.

a silhouette against the backdrop of despair,
caught in the undertow of self-comparison's
snare.
in this verse of sorrow, I quietly fade,
lost in the shadows of a self I've betrayed.

lost in the verse

in the midst of collegiate ambition,
I stepped into the realm of creative expression.
full of dreams, I embraced the challenge,
believing my words would soar on wings of
inspiration.

but soon, I became entangled
in the dense thicket of literary theory,
each concept a maze, each symbol a puzzle.
lost in the intricacy of interpretation,
I struggled to find my way.

workshops became battlegrounds,
where my ego clashed with unyielding critique.
exposed and vulnerable,
I faced the scrutiny of my peers,
questioning the worth of my voice.

in moments of doubt, I turned
to the giants of literature,
seeking solace in their brilliance.
yet their towering achievements
only cast shadows on my own aspirations.

now, I stand on the precipice of academia,
a failed pilgrim in the land of creativity.
yet amidst the rubble of shattered dreams,
I cling to the hope that somewhere,
in the chaos of my words,
there lies a story waiting to be told.

whispers in water

in the quiet sanctuary of porcelain walls,
I've perfected the art of a swift, silent
unraveling.
with practiced ease, I slip away from prying
eyes,
finding solace in the cool embrace of solitude.

a deft flick of the faucet, a gentle splash of
water,
and I'm cocooned in a private symphony of
release.
tears flow freely, unchecked by judgment or
restraint,
each droplet a testament to the weight I carry.

there's a certain liberation in this hidden
sanctuary,

where vulnerability is not weakness but
resilience.
in the echo of my own sobs, I find strength,
a reminder that even in darkness, there is light.

so I let the tears fall, unburdening my soul,
embracing the raw beauty of my humanity.
for in this transient moment of surrender,
I find healing in the simple act of letting go.

8 AM

in the vast expanse of tedium,
I find myself wandering aimlessly,
lost amidst the tumbleweeds of monotony,
in search of a spark to ignite the desert of
boredom.

restlessness whispers in my ear,
a persistent companion on this journey,
as I navigate the barren landscape,
hoping for a glimpse of something more.

but fear not, for I've become quite the explorer,
a seasoned traveler in this wasteland of ennui,
where every step is a quest for diversion,
and every sigh is met with a shrug from the
universe.

oops I forgot it again

in the haze of days blending into one another,
I find myself slipping,
lost in the perplexity of routine,
forgetting the lifeline that keeps me afloat.

slowly, imperceptibly at first,
but then with gathering momentum,
I spiral into the depths,
drowning in the undertow of my own mind.

each day becomes a struggle,
a battle against the weight of existence,
as I grapple with the shadows,
desperate for a glimmer of light.

but in the darkness, there is a flicker,
a tiny ember of hope,
guiding me back to the surface,
where I can breathe again.

and so, with hesitant steps,
I begin the journey anew,
tracing my way back to stability,
one small victory at a time.

sinking shadows

in the depths of my mind,
I find myself tangled in the threads of thought,
each one a knot tightening around my limbs,
binding me to the depths of despair.

I spiral downward, deeper and deeper,
lost in the catacombs of my own creation,
as the weight of worry presses down,
crushing my spirit beneath its heavy burden.

and there, in the darkness,
I lay entombed in my own inertia,
unable to muster the strength to rise,
held captive by the gravity of my own thoughts.

the world outside fades into oblivion,
as I sink further into the abyss,
trapped in a cycle of overthinking,

unable to break free from its suffocating
embrace.

and so I remain, a prisoner of my own mind,
hostage in the darkness of my thoughts,
longing for the light of hope to pierce the gloom,
and lead me back to the surface once more.

it's always the quencher girlies, am I right

in the palm of my hand, a silent companion,
a vessel of solace, cool against my skin,
its presence a balm to my weary soul,
a silent witness to my unspoken woes.

with each grasp, I draw comfort,
as if its very touch could soothe the ache within,
an anchor in the storm of emotion,
a steady presence amidst the chaos of life.

in its embrace, I find refuge,
a sanctuary from the tumultuous world outside,
its weight a reminder of the strength within,
a silent testament to resilience and grace.

and so, I hold onto it tightly,
a lifeline in times of need,
an emotional support in physical form,
a source of comfort and calm in a turbulent sea.

canvas of connection

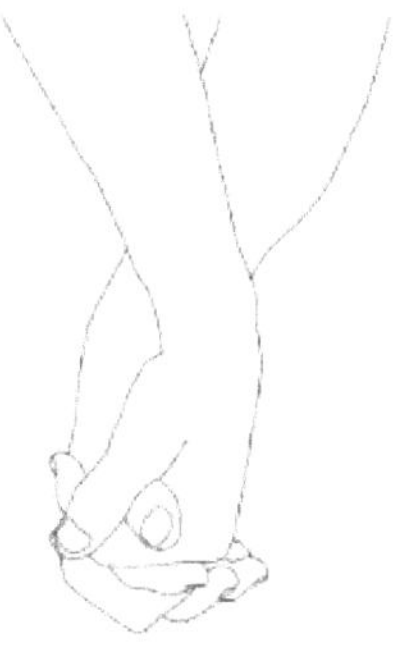

in the tapestry of our shared experiences,
I navigate the threads of your passions,
each one a colorful hue in the mosaic of your
soul.

but amidst the swirl of interests and pursuits,
there are moments when I find myself adrift,
caught in the currents of your enthusiasm,
yet struggling to find my footing.

it's not that I don't appreciate your fervor,
or admire the depth of your dedication,
but there are times when our paths diverge,
and I'm left feeling like a traveler in unfamiliar
terrain.

yet even in these moments of disconnect,
there's a comfort in knowing that our differences
are but brushstrokes on the canvas of our
relationship,
adding depth and texture to the masterpiece we
create together.

lost in life's symphony

in the sprawling saga of human existence,
I am but a footnote,
a minor character in the grand narrative of life,
lost in the shuffle of billions of souls.

surrounded by the cacophony of voices,
each one clamoring for attention,
I struggle to make my own heard,
drowned out by the roar of the crowd.

I watch as others blaze trails of glory,
their names etched in the annals of history,
while I linger in the shadows,
a mere spectator to their triumphs.

I am the architect of my own deception,
crafting a facade of contentment,
while inside, I am consumed by doubt,

and plagued by the fear of inadequacy.

with each passing moment,
I feel the weight of expectation bearing down,
pressing me into the earth like a heavy stone,
until I am buried beneath its crushing weight.

but still, I soldier on,
a brave face masking my inner turmoil,
as I navigate the treacherous waters of life,
in search of a beacon to guide me home.

I tell myself that I am happy,
that I am exactly where I want to be,
but the truth is far more complicated,
a tangled web of dreams and aspirations.

I long to break free from the chains of
conformity,
to carve out a path uniquely my own,
but fear holds me back,
its tendrils coiling around my heart like a
serpent.

so I remain trapped in the prison of my own
making,
a captive to circumstance,
hoping for a sign,
a glimmer of hope to light my way forward.

catastrophe comrades

in the fabric of our shared existence,
there are shadows that linger, unnoticed,
moments of turmoil that shape our intertwined
journey,
and challenges that test the essence of our
connection.

through the storms that silently brew,
and the trials that quietly unfold,
we find solace in the subtle solidarity,
drawing strength from the invisible threads
between us.

in the fleeting glances exchanged,
and the unspoken gestures of understanding,
we discover a bond that transcends words,

nurtured by the intangible ties that bind us.

with each obstacle, we navigate,
our bond deepens, a silent testament,
to the endurance of our relationship,
and the timeless resonance of our shared history.

though the scars of our past may remain veiled,
they serve as reminders of the hurdles
surmounted,
and the victories celebrated together,
a testament to the depth of our connection.

in the symphony of life's mysteries,
your presence is an ethereal melody,
a guiding force in the midst of uncertainty,
and for that, my dear, you're an absolute angel.

in the intricate tapestry of our intertwined
destinies,
your essence weaves through every fiber,
a testament to the beauty of our bond,
and the timeless grace of our connection.

incompetent valve

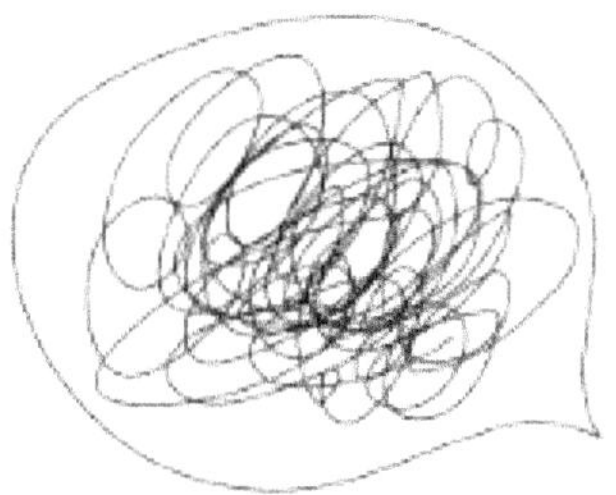

in the shadowed chamber of academia,
a lone figure presides with an air of mystery,
their discourse a maze of ambiguity,
leaving us adrift in a haze of uncertainty.

I strain to unravel their cryptic narrative,
but it slips through my grasp like an elusive
mist,
leaving me lost in a maze of conjecture,
wandering aimlessly through corridors of
confusion.

the gestures are a dance of intrigue,
their meaning shrouded in veils of obscurity,
as if orchestrating a clandestine ritual,
in a tongue known only to the initiated.

I exchange subtle glances with my companions,
our expressions a silent symphony of perplexity,
as we navigate the shadowy depths of the
lecture,
seeking glimpses of insight amidst the murk.

beyond these walls, the world beckons with its
secrets,
but here we remain, ensnared in this enigma,
a captive audience to the professor's enigmatic
performance,
yearning for the elusive spark of illumination.

in the quiet of goodbye

in the quiet moments before dawn,
when the world slumbers in peaceful oblivion,
I find myself wrestling with the weight of
goodbyes,
a heavy burden that settles like a stone in my
chest.

for farewell is no easy task,
it is a bittersweet symphony of emotions,
a delicate dance between joy and sorrow,
as we bid adieu to what once was, and what
could have been.

the curls of nostalgia wrap around me,
a gentle reminder of the memories we shared,
the laughter that echoed through the halls,
and the tears that stained our cheeks.

but with each goodbye comes the promise of
new beginnings,
a glimmer of hope amidst the darkness,
as we step bravely into the unknown,
leaving behind the familiar comforts of the past.

yet moving on is not without its challenges,
it is a leap of faith into the abyss,
a journey into uncharted territory,
where uncertainty looms like a specter on the
horizon.

the fear of the unknown gnaws at my soul,
a relentless adversary that taunts and teases,
as I stand on the precipice of change,
wondering what lies beyond the horizon.

but amidst the fear and uncertainty,
there is a quiet resilience that stirs within,
a flicker of determination that refuses to be
extinguished,
as I take the first tentative steps towards
tomorrow.

so goodbye, my dear friend,
though parting is sweet sorrow,
I carry your memory with me,
as I embark on this journey called life.

once more with feeling

in the aftermath of loss, chaos reigns supreme,
a tempest of emotions swirling within,
anger pulses through my veins, a fiery torrent,
as I rail against the injustice of it all,
fists clenched, teeth gritted, I scream into the
void,
demanding answers that will never come.

bargaining follows, a desperate plea,
to turn back the hands of time,
to rewrite the script of our shared existence,
to undo the damage that has been done,
but the universe remains unmoved,
indifferent to our cries.

depression descends like a heavy blanket,
smothering me with its suffocating weight,
as I drown in a sea of sorrow and regret,

lost in the darkness of my own mind,
I struggle to find solid ground,
in a world that suddenly feels unsteady.

acceptance comes last, a bitter pill to swallow,
as I resign myself to the harsh reality,
that nothing will ever be the same again,
that the person I loved is gone forever,
and all that remains is an empty void,
a gaping wound that will never fully heal.

but even as I come to terms with the loss,
I am haunted by the echoes of what could have
been,
the memories of a life cut short,
and the pain of a future forever altered.

in the end, there is only emptiness,
a vast expanse of nothingness,
stretching out before me into eternity,
as I grapple with the harsh reality,
of a world without you.

always know just how much I adore you

always know just how much I adore you,
for in the depths of my soul, your memory
resides,
a cherished treasure, a beacon of light,
guiding me through the darkness of my days.

but forgiveness is a heavy burden to bear,
a weight that presses down on my heart,
as I grapple with the pain of your absence,
and the wounds that remain unhealed.

they say time heals all wounds,
But what they don't tell you is that some
wounds,
run so deep, they become a part of you,
a constant reminder of the pain that once was.

I try to find solace in forgiveness,
to let go of the anger and resentment that binds
me,
but every time I reach out, I find myself,
clutching onto the hurt like a lifeline.

how do you forgive someone who is no longer
here?
how do you make peace with the past,
when the one you need to forgive is gone,
leaving behind a trail of unanswered questions?

I wish I could say that forgiveness comes easy,
that I can simply let go of the pain and move on,
but the truth is, it's not that simple,
and maybe it never will be.

so for now, all I can do is hold onto the love,
the memories that sustain me in your absence,
and hope that someday, forgiveness will come,
and I can finally let go of the pain that binds me.

but until then, always know just how much I
adore you,
for in the end, love is all that remains,
a thread that connects us across time and space,
and keeps you forever close to my heart.

9 789360 946807